Francis Roberts

On the moral law and judicial law

Francis Roberts

On the moral law and judicial law

ISBN/EAN: 9783744646673

Printed in Europe, USA, Canada, Australia, Japan

Cover: Foto ©Suzi / pixelio.de

More available books at **www.hansebooks.com**

On the Moral Law and Judicial Law

Francis Roberts

1675

Being Book 3, Chapter 4, Aphorism 1, Question 2, Section 3 of his

The Mystery and Marrow of the Bible: God's Covenants with Man

Table of Contents

Introduction

Francis Roberts (1609-1675) wrote the puritan *magnum opus* on covenant theology. The importance that Roberts attached to this subject is reflected both in the book's size of 1700 pages and in its title: The Mystery and Marrow of the Bible: God's Covenants with Man (1675). Roberts understood covenant theology to comprise the marrow, or heart, of the Bible.

Of peculiar interest in this work for today is Roberts' section on the Law of Moses. On the one hand, there are Christians who believe that the whole Moral Law in Moses is done away and that Christians need not be directed by it. On the other hand, there are other Christians ('Messianic Jews') that try to keep the Ceremonial Law. They both agree that the whole Mosaic Law stands or falls together.

Roberts, representing historic Christianity, distinguishes the Mosaic Law into three categories: (1) the Moral Law (the Ten Commandments), (2) the Ceremonial Law (all the laws relating to the sacrifices), and (3) the Judicial Law (the civil laws of Israel). Roberts then demonstrates this three-fold distinction from scripture and gives five grounds for the superiority of the Moral Law:

(1) The Moral Law alone was spoken audibly by God on Mt. Sinai (compare Dt. 5:22 with Ex. 20:1,19,21; 21:1);

(2) The Moral Law alone was written by the finger of God upon two tables (Ex. 31:18) and kept in the symbol of God's presence, the ark of the covenant;

(3) The Moral Law is the foundation of the Ceremonial and Judicial Laws;

(4) The Moral Law alone was written on the heart of Adam and all of his posterity;

(5) The Moral Law alone is of perpetually binding moral obligation upon all people in all ages.

Respecting the Judicial Law, on the one hand, there are Christians today (antinomians) who believe it has no relevance today. On the other hand, there are Christian Theonomists who believe that the Judicial Law in whole binds civil rulers 'in exhaustive detail'. Roberts, reflecting the Westminster Confession (1646) and the majority consensus of puritanism, held that the Judicial Laws have expired with the cessation of the polity of Israel, though their general equity (the Moral Law that undergirds them) continues to bind civil rulers today. The wisdom and equity of the laws of a Christian magistrate, Roberts says, will "notably appear by comparing them in some due analogy with these [Judicial Laws] of God Himself, which were the most wise, full and righteous political laws that ever were contrived."[1]

Roberts also notes (in accordance with Westminster Confession, chapter 23, 1646) that the civil magistrate is to uphold in his jurisdiction not just the second table of the law (those commands primarily concerned with crimes against man), but the whole Moral Law, that is, all the Ten Commandments, including the commandments of the first table of the law (which primarily concern crimes against God).

Roberts' section on the Ceremonial Law (10 pages) has been omitted from this edition. May this work be a blessing and instructive to you as you meditate upon God's Law day and night (Ps. 1:2).

Rev. Travis Fentiman, MDiv., 2015
of the Free Church of Scotland (Continuing)

---

[1] *On the Moral Law and Judicial Law*, p. 23

3

III. Of the Distribution or Division of God's Law Given to Moses and to Israel on Mt. Sinai

God's Law given to Moses and Israel on Mt. Sinai is, in respect of the subject matter therein contained, most usually divided into three sorts, namely: Moral, Ceremonial, and Judicial. Or, if we rather affect a dichotomy, into two sorts. That is:

1. Perpetual, of obligatory force and power forever, as the Moral Law contained in Ten Commandments.

2. Temporary, of obligatory power and force only for a certain time, and then determinable. And this concerning (1) the worship and service of God, as the Ceremonial Law, and (2) the civil state and polity of the Jews, as the Judicial Law. Both of which were to determine and expire after the death of Christ, Christ being the substance or body of those shadows (the accomplishment of those ceremonies and the commonwealth of the Jews, not long after Christ's death, being utterly dissolved).

The word 'moral' in the general notation of it, is that which appertains to manners, directs and obliges about manners, etc. And in that latitude it is applicable both to the ceremonial and judicial laws which are in some sense commanded in the moral law, though they be not perpetual but temporary only.

But in this distinction by the word 'moral', I understand such laws touching manners as are always binding, and therein are opposed to ceremonial and judicial laws binding only for a time. And in this sense we may receive this distinction without scruple.

For the further clearing [explaining] of it, I shall show:

I. That this common distinction has its foundation in scripture.

II. What the nature was of these three sorts of laws.

III. That they were all delivered by God to Moses on Mt. Sinai for Israel.[2]

I. That This Distinction of God's Law into Moral, Ceremonial and Judicial is Founded on Scripture

This is evident:

1. By testimonies of Moses, which frequently enumerate these three branches, as:

> 'The Lord spoke unto you out of the midst of the fire... and He declared unto you his Covenant, which He commanded you to perform, even Ten Commandments (in Hebrew: 'ten words') and He wrote them upon two tables of stone. And the Lord commanded me at that time to teach you statutes, and judgments, that you might do them in the land whither you go over to possess it.' (Deut. 4:12-14)

Here, by 'Ten Words' (or ten brief sentences by way of command, properly ten sayings, as the Hebrew signifies) understand, the Moral Law

---

[2] This edition of 'On the Moral Law and Judicial Law' ends at the end of Part II and does not include Part III.

summarily comprised in the Ten Commandments. By 'statutes' understand the Ceremonial Law, and by 'judgments' the Judicial or political law. And these are here expressly distinguished, both by their variety of denominations and by their difference of dispensation, the Moral Law being written by God, but not the Ceremonial and Judicial.

Sometimes they are expressed by 'commandments, statutes, and judgments' (Deut. 4:1; 6:1; 7:11; 8:11; 11:1; 26:17; 30:16; Lev. 26:14). Sometimes by 'laws, statutes, and judgments': 'These are the statutes and judgments and laws, which the Lord made between Him and the children of Israel in Mt. Sinai by the hand of Moses.' (Lev. 26:46) Sometimes by 'testimonies, statutes, and judgments' (Deut. 6:20). All to the same effect for substance: denoting the Moral, Ceremonial, and Judicial Laws.

2. By the testimony of Malachi. 'Remember ye the law of Moses my servant, which I commanded unto him in Horeb for all Israel, the statutes, and judgments.' (Mal. 4:4) Here's law, statutes, and judgments, as formerly.

3. By the testimony of Paul. 'Who are Israelites: to whom pertains the adoption, and the glory, and the covenants (or testaments), and the giving of the law, and the service of God, and the promises.' (Rom. 9:4) To omit vain curiosities in interpreting these particulars, this sense of them seems to me most genuine:

'The glory', namely, the ark of God, elsewhere called 'the glory' (1 Sam. 4:21,22).

'The covenants', namely, the two tables of the Covenant, which were put into that ark and there reserved. Here is the Moral Law.

6

'The giving of the law', namely, the constituting of Judicial and political laws for that commonwealth.

'The service of God', namely, that manner of God's service and worship which was prescribed in the Ceremonial Law for that people till Christ should come in the flesh.

I leave it to the judgment of discreet minds whether this be not the true intent of the apostle. And if so, then here's the Law distinguished into these three sorts.

II. What the Nature was of These Three Sorts of Laws

To unfold their nature particularly and individually would require a vast volume of itself. It shall suffice as to my present purpose to give only a small taste of these three laws more generally.

I. Of the Moral Law

The Moral Law has the singular preeminence above both the others in many regards:

1. That alone being uttered by the voice of God to all Israel from Mt. Sinai (Dt. 5:22).

2. That alone being twice written in tables of stone by the finger of God. First, in tables of God's own preparing which were broken, and never put into the ark (Dt. 4:13; Ex. 31:18; 32:16,19). Secondly, in tables of Moses' preparing, which were not broken but were reserved in the ark (Ex. 34:1,4).

3. That alone being the base and foundation of the other two; which [Ceremonials and Judicials] reductively are referred to the Moral Law as particular additions thereunto, and explanations thereof for the condition and continuance of the Jewish Church and commonwealth.

But the Ceremonial and Judicial Laws are in no sense the foundation of the Moral Law. For, as one well observes[3], the Ceremonial and Judicial Laws are nothing else but special appendices to the Moral Law, rivulets [small streams] derived from the fountain of piety and equity, special ordinances peculiarly concerning the Jewish church and commonwealth. The Ceremonial Laws are the exercises of the first table, determining the worship of God prescribed in the first table by external circumstances. The Judicial Laws are the exercises of the second table, determining in like sort righteousness towards men prescribed in the second table by outward circumstances. Yea, upon this Moral Law hang all the Law and the Prophets (Matt 22:40).

4. That alone, in all the branches of it, conforms and is answerable to the Law of Nature written in Adam's heart at

---

[3] John Gerhard, in location, Of the Ceremonial Law, I. Gerhard (1582-1637) was a Lutheran from Germany.

his creation (the Ceremonial Law being merely positive and instituted, revealing only God's instituted worship and typifying only supernatural mysteries in Christ Jesus; the Judicial Law being only of positive institution for that commonwealth of the Jews and obliging formally as such no other commonwealth in the world thereunto, though the matter of some Judicials, so far as bottomed upon moral principles and foundations, may also analogically oblige other godly and Christian commonwealths).

5. That alone being of perpetual force and power to all the churches of God in all succeeding ages both under Old and New Testament. For, the Ceremonial Laws vanished at Christ's death, having received their accomplishment in Him, and the Judicials expired at the dissolution of the Jewish commonwealth. In these and like respects, the Moral Law far excels the Ceremonial and Judicial.

The Moral Law has diverse denominations. It is called:

1. 'The Law', or 'a Law,' (Ex. 24:12) by way of eminency, as being the Law of laws.

2. 'The Law of the Lord', or 'The Law of God', 'I will put my Law in their inward parts,' (Jer. 31:33) from the principal Author and Lawgiver thereof.

3. 'The Law of Moses,' (Mal. 4:4) from the instrument used by the Lord in giving it.

9

4. 'A fiery law,' (Dt. 33:2; 5:22) in Hebrew: 'a fire of Law,' from the manner of God's promulgating it out of the midst of the fire, of the cloud, and of the thick darkness, with a great voice.

5. 'The Commandment', or precept. 'Now these are the Commandment, the Statutes, and the Judgments.' (Dt. 6:1) Commandment, or precept, is in the singular number for commandments in the plural, by an enallage [grammatical interchange] of the number. Or, because all the commandments are comprised in that one great commandment: Love.

6. 'Words,' (Ex. 20:1; Dt. 5:22) because God spoke and uttered them with a great voice, in the hearing of all Israel.

7. 'Ten words.' (Dt. 4:13) We render it, 'Ten Commandments,' that is, ten brief commanding sentences touching ten distinct sorts of duties.

8. 'The Testimony of the Lord' (Ps. 19:7; Ex. 25:16,21; 31:18), partly because it testifies as a record what is God's will and the mystery of his counsels (Jn. 5:39), partly because of the earnest testification, contestation and charge given by God and his prophets concerning the observance of it (as Dt. 31:28; 32:4; Ps. 81:9; 2 Kings 17:15; Neh. 9:29,30).

9. 'God's Covenant,' because it was delivered on Mt. Sinai in the notion and formality of a covenant, and as it was one

of the eminent dispensations of God's Covenant of Faith,[4] as after shall appear in its due place.

10. 'Covenants,' (Rom. 9:4) in reference to the two tables wherein this Covenant was written, etc.

These and like denominations tend something to clear [explain] the nature of this Moral Law.

The Moral Law and the nature thereof will further receive much light from a due distribution thereof into its several heads and branches. Now there are three sorts of divisions or distributions of the Law observable and useful to this end, namely:

1. Into two tables.

2. Into Ten Words, or Ten Commandments.

3. Into rules of love to God and to man.

The first of these arises from the subject containing the Law, that is, the two tables of stone wherein God wrote this Law twice with his own finger. The second, from the summary heads or kinds of arguments contained in the Law, which are evidently ten. The third, from the scope and end of the Law, which is love, and from the mutual connection or dependence of those duties or acts of love to, or upon, one another.

---

[4] ['Covenant of Faith' in Roberts' usage correlates to the Old Testament administrations of the Covenant of Grace.]

1. First, the Law is divided into two tables. This distribution has God's own authority for it. The Lord Himself divided his Law into two general branches by writing it in two distinct tables of stone (Dt. 4:13), once and again: the one table containing duties to God, as a table of holiness; the other table containing duties to man, as a table of righteousness. The Lord could as easily have written his whole Law upon one table, but He would distinguish his laws into two general heads according to their two sorts of objects: God and man.

2. Secondly, the Law is divided into Ten Words. 'And He declared unto you his Covenant, which He commanded you to perform *hashereth haddebarim,* 'ten words,' and He wrote them upon two tables of stone (Dt. 4:13). This distribution also is of divine authority. By 'ten words' understand not only ten individual words and no more, but (as the Hebrew phrase may well be interpreted) ten sayings, or ten speeches, namely: ten commanding sayings, comprised in ten distinct compendious sentences, aphorisms, or periods, touching ten distinct matters or duties. Hence, in Greek they are called, 'the Decalogue.' These Ten Commandments were written in the two tables. But how many were written in the one and how many in the other, is controverted. Here I find chiefly three opinions:

> 1. The Jews refer five to one table and five to another, adding the fifth commandment to the first table, because superiors and rulers are called 'gods' (Ps. 82:6). But this ground is weak. For,

inferiors are also comprehended in this fifth commandment and they are not stiled 'gods.' Besides, this fifth commandment immediately respects man, not God. Now our Savior refers all the commandments immediately respecting God to the love of God, and all the commandments immediately respecting man to the love of our neighbor (Lk. 10:27,28; Mt. 22:36-39). Therefore doubtless God the wise Lawgiver did so distinguish them in the two tables.

2. The papists[5] refer but three commandments to the first table, making the first and second commandment all one (through the subtlety of Satan that the making and worshipping of any images except images of God may seem the less palpably to be condemned). And they add seven to the second table, dividing the last commandment into two so that they may make up the number ten. And Gerhard notes[6] that all Lutherans who sincerely follow the Augustane Confession[7] and Luther's Catechism embrace this division. Now this division (though it distinctly ranks all the commandments touching holiness to one table and all the commandments touching righteousness to the other) yet, is liable to very just exception. For, it conjoins the first and second commandments into one (which are

---

[5] Jerome Zanchius, *Of the Decalogue*, Book 1, Ch. 11, Thesis 4

[6] John Gerhard, in location, *Commentary on the Law of God*, Ch. 4, Section 6, Paragraph 43

[7] [This is the Latin name for the Lutheran Augsburg Confession, 1530]

of a quite different sense and intention) and it divides the last commandment into two (both which have the same scope and meaning). Both of them seem to brag that this also was Augustine's judgment.[8] I grant, it was Augustine's judgment. But his ground for it (namely, the insinuating hereby the trinity of persons in the Godhead), says Dr. Andrews,[9] was very weak. Zanchy says:[10] was childish.

3. The orthodox protestant writers embrace the best distribution: referring the four first commandments (touching religion and holiness towards God) to the first table and the six last (touching righteousness towards man) to the second table.

> 1. Hereby they avoid all the inconveniences of the former divisions.

> 2. Hereby they do most properly rank all the commandments touching religion to the first table and all the commandments touching righteousness to the second.

> 3. Hereby the first and great commandment of loving God is rightly ordered before the second of loving man (this being subordinate to that and depending thereupon).

---

[8] Augustine, *Confessions*, Book 3, Ch. 8, and Question 71 in *Exodus*
[9] Andrews, *On the Ten Commandments*, p. 105-106, London, 1642
[10] Jerome Zanchius, *Of the Decalogue*, Book 1, Ch. 11, Thesis 4

3. Thirdly, the Law is divided in reference to the matter and scope of it (which is love, 1 Tim. 1:5), into two great commandments, namely: the first, To Love the Lord our God with all our heart, soul, mind and might; and, the second, To love our neighbor as ourselves. This is our blessed Savior's distribution (Matt 22:36-41), and therefore it is of divine authority also. Love to God comprises all the duties of religion towards God in the first table; love to our neighbor comprehending all duties of righteousness towards man, in the second table.

Under these two general heads, we may thus rank all the ten commandments according to this ensuing scheme, namely:

The matter and scope of the Moral Law is love (1 Tim. 1:5).

I. Love to God, comprising all duties of religion, piety, holiness, or of the worship of God, which are prescribed in the first table, and condemning all contrary sins, wherein the Lord teaches:

1. Who is to be had and worshipped as our God, namely, Jehovah alone, the only true God in Christ (1st Commandment).

2. How this only true God Jehovah is to be worshipped.

3. Both when and at what special times the Lord our God is to be more solemnly worshipped, namely, on his Sabbath days (which are to be devoted, and sanctified to God's

worship and service peculiarly, under the New Testament as well as under the Old). (4th Commandment)

   1. In his solemn or set worship, whether public or private, namely, that this true God Jehovah will be worshiped only by such means and in such manner as He Himself has appointed in his Word. (2nd Commandment)

   2. In our whole course of life, namely, that in all things, throughout the same, we sanctify and glorify his Name, that is, everything whereby He makes Himself known (even as man is known by his name). (3rd Commandment)

II. Love to our neighbor, comprising all duties of sobriety, equity and righteousness, which are prescribed in the second table, and the condemning of all opposite vices. These duties and vices are:

   1. Of more peculiar concernment to persons as in relation of superiors, equals, and inferiors, and that in all sorts of societies, political, ecclesiastical, domestical. (5th Commandment)

   2. Of a more general and common concernment to all persons.

Here vices are forbidden, which:

   1. Have the will's consent to act them, and this against our neighbors.

2. Go before the will's deliberate and actual consent (as concupiscence), or, are the first motions of the heart, against our neighbor's good in any respect (10th Commandment):

1. Their person, life, health, etc. (6th Commandment)

2. Their purity or chastity. (7th Commandment)

3. Their possessions or outward enjoyments. (8th Commandment)

4. Their good name. (9th Commandment)

Thus the matter and end of the whole Moral Law, jointly and of every of the Ten Commandments severally, is so far discovered in a more general way as to let us see:

1. How holy, just, and good the Law is (Rom. 7:12);

2. How spiritual, and heavenly it is (Rom. 7:14);

3. How soul searching, heart penetrating, and convincing it is (Rom. 7:7);

4. How large, comprehensive, and complete it is, reaching to all sorts, sexes and degrees of persons, regulating all sorts and degrees of actions, words, thoughts and imaginations, and condemning all sinful failings in them all together, with all the circumstances and aggravations thereof (Ps. 119:96).

Thus of the Moral Law.

[II. Of the Ceremonial Law, 10 pages, is omitted]

III. Of the Judicial Law

The Judicial Law was added by God as an appendix to his Moral Law and it regulated the people of the Jews (as now to be digested and formed into a politic body, civil state, or commonwealth) in the exercise of all acts of equity, righteousness, and sobriety, towards themselves and one another, being prescribed in the commandments of the second table especially. Notwithstanding some of them also had reference to acts of piety and religion in the first table, with civil mulcts [penalties] punishing offences, etc., contrary thereunto.

The Lord Himself was the supreme Monarch, King, Judge, Ruler, Governor and Lawgiver of this commonwealth peculiarly. He formed them into a commonwealth. He gave them the best political laws that ever any commonwealth had. He from time to time set rulers and governors of several sorts over them. Their political constitution was monarchical, aristocratic, and democratic, and therefore most prudently and perfectly composed:

> 1. Monarchical, in that God would still have it governed by one person as supreme (Acts 7:30,35; Numb. 27:16-18, etc.; Acts 13:20-21), first by Moses, then by Joshua, then judges, then by kings, then by princes and governors after

the captivity. The raising up and erecting of which supreme rulers, God reserved still to Himself as Supreme over all.

2. Aristocratic, in that seventy chief, wise, understanding, and known men among their tribes were as princes set over them as assistants to the supreme governor Moses, etc. (Dt. 1:9-10,19)

3. Democratic, in that these chief heads were chosen by the people themselves out of every tribe (Dt. 1:13, etc).

This was the form of their polity, the best form, and most excellently composed for preventing of anarchy, popular confusions and divisions, arbitrariness, and tyranny.

These Judicial Laws are stiled:

1. Most usually *mishphatim,* 'judgments' (Dt. 4:14,45; 6:1; 7:11; 8:11; 11:1; 26:17; 30:16; Mal.4:4), because they were the wise and righteous determinations or judgments of God for their commonwealth, and were to be a standing rule for all their judgments, sentences and proceedings in their civil courts of judicature. So the Greek calls them, *judgments.*

2. Sometimes *hedouth,* 'testimonies': 'And made a covenant before the Lord to walk after the Lord, and to keep his commandments and his testimonies and statutes, with all his heart, and with all his soul' (2 Chron. 34:31). So called, because these judicials were testifications of God's will and pleasure, how He would have that commonwealth guided and their judicial proceedings ordered.

3. Sometimes 'the legislation', or 'giving of the Law' (Rom. 9:4), which (being in this enumeration of Jewish privileges contradistinct from 'the covenants', namely, the two tables of Covenant, containing the Moral Law, and from the service of God, directed in the Ceremonial Law) seems plainly and particularly to intend the Judicial Law, and not generally the giving of the whole Law.

Judicial Laws may variously be divided or distributed:

1. According to the extent of right into laws concerning persons, things or actions.

2. According to the four ranks and relations of persons or people in every well ordered commonwealth, namely:

1. Rulers and subjects;

2. Subjects and subjects;

3. Family relations, that is, between husband and wife, parents and children, masters and servants;

4. Subjects and foreigners.

Thus that clear and learned Zanchius marshals all the Judicials [into these two categories].[11] But these two ways of dividing the Judicials seem too narrow and not adequate to them: forasmuch as there are diverse Judicials that have

---

[11] Jerome Zanchius, *de Led. De.*, Book 1, Chapter 10, Thesis 6

reference to offences against the first table (though most of them concern the second table).

3. According to the Ten Commandments contained in both tables. God has made the civil magistrate *custodem utrius[que] tabulae*, keeper and guardian of both the tables, having commanded him to inflict civil mulcts and penalties upon transgressors of the first, as well as of the second table.

Thus that excellent and judicious Calvin, distributing the matter of those four books of Moses (Exodus, Leviticus, Numbers and Deuteronomy) into historical and doctrinal [categories], harmoniously refers all the doctrinals therein to one body, namely, all the Ceremonials and Judicials to the Ten Commandments of the Moral Law for the more clear explaining and understanding of them.[12] To which (for brevity's sake) I refer the learned reader, as being a very useful and advantageous work. Gerhard also refers the Judicials to the Ten Commandments,[13] but herein wrongs his references in that he follows the corrupt Popish distribution of the Ten Commandments fore-rejected.

Now the Lord imposed not these Judicials upon the gentiles, but only upon the Jews during the continuance of their commonwealth. Nor are Christian commonwealths now under the New Testament formally under those laws or obliged by them,

---

[12] John Calvin, *Harmony of the Books of Moses*, and *Commentary on Exodus*, Chapter 20
[13] John Gerhard, *Commentary on the Law*, Tract. 3, Chapter 2

further than the moral ground and equity thereof binds analogically.[14] God gave these Judicial Laws to the Jews:

> 1. That, He might hereby let them see that He Himself immediately was their King, their Judge, their Lawgiver, and they immediately his subjects and people, having no other supreme magistrate, whether king, judge, or lawgiver over them besides God alone when these laws were first given.

> 2. That there might be the form of a well ordered commonwealth in Israel wherein vice might be suppressed, virtue encouraged, necessary political union and communion established for their mutual strengthening, defense, support and comfort, and that they might live like men, not beasts: like religious men, not pagans.

> 3. That, they might perceive how much God approves of government, order, public peace, honesty, righteousness, distinction of things, etc., and how much He abhors anarchy, confusion, tyranny, barbarousness, injustice, etc.

> 4. That they might know how great a rewarder God was of all piety and righteousness and how severe an avenger of all sin and wickedness.

> 5. That in this well constituted and well regulated commonwealth the church and ordinances of God might have quiet, safe and comfortable subsistence.

---

[14] [See point 6 below for what Roberts means by this.]

Commonwealths are the church's and gospel's receptacles, without the good composure and government whereof the church cannot long be, or not be well.

6. That God might proportionally instruct all Christian magistrates under the New Testament to govern their subjects by wise and righteous laws made known unto the people and not arbitrarily by their own mere will and pleasure. The wisdom and equity of whose laws will notably appear by comparing them in some due analogy with these of God Himself, which were the most wise, full and righteous political laws that ever were contrived.

Thus of the Judicial Law.

The End

9 783744 646673